Benefits Of No Treat Dog Training And Puppy Training

Training your dog is an essential part of responsible pet ownership, and it brings numerous benefits for both you and your furry friend. While traditional treat-based training has long been popular, an alternative approach called no treat dog training is gaining recognition. This technique focuses on positive reinforcement without relying on food rewards, leading to a more balanced and harmonious relationship between you and your canine companion. In this article, we'll explore the benefits of no treat dog training and puppy training, providing insights into why this approach can be highly effective in shaping your dog's behavior and enhancing your bond.

CONTENTS

INTRODUCTION

Dog training plays a crucial role in helping our canine friends become well-behaved members of society. It teaches them obedience, appropriate behavior, and necessary skills for daily life. No treat dog training, also known as reward-based or positive reinforcement training, is a modern approach that emphasizes the use of positive reinforcement methods without the heavy reliance on treats. This method can be particularly effective for puppies and dogs that are sensitive to food or have specific dietary restrictions.

BUILDING A STRONG BOND

One of the significant benefits of no treat dog training is its ability to foster a strong bond between you and your dog. By focusing on positive reinforcement techniques, this approach allows you to build trust, respect, and understanding with your furry companion. Rather than relying solely on treats,

you establish a foundation of communication, cooperation, and mutual respect, which forms the basis of a healthy and fulfilling relationship.

Positive reinforcement techniques involve rewarding desirable behavior with praise, affection, and playtime. When your dog realizes that their actions result in positive outcomes, they become more inclined to repeat those behaviors. This creates a positive feedback loop that deepens your bond and encourages your dog to actively engage and participate in the training process.

POSITIVE REINFORCEMENT TECHNIQUES

No treat dog training relies on various positive reinforcement techniques that can be highly effective in shaping your dog's behavior. Instead of offering food rewards, you can employ methods such as clicker training, verbal praise, affectionate petting, or interactive play as positive reinforcers.

Clicker training is a popular technique that involves using a handheld clicker to mark desired behaviors, followed by a reward or praise. The sound of the clicker serves as a clear and consistent signal, helping your dog understand exactly which actions are being reinforced. This method is often employed during obedience training, teaching your dog to associate specific commands with positive outcomes.

Verbal praise and affection are powerful tools in no treat dog training. Dogs are highly responsive to the tone and enthusiasm in our voices, and praising them with a cheerful "Good boy!" or a gentle pat on the head can be incredibly reinforcing. The bond between you and your dog strengthens as you shower them with love and appreciation for their efforts.

Rewarding your dog with playtime can be an excellent alternative to treat-based rewards. Interactive play sessions not only provide physical exercise and mental stimulation but also serve as a valuable opportunity to reinforce positive behaviors. Whether it's a game of fetch, tug-of-war, or a playful romp in the park, engaging in enjoyable activities together strengthens the bond and reinforces desired behaviors.

PROMOTING SELF-DISCIPLINE

No treat dog training encourages the development of self-discipline in your dog. By teaching them impulse control and fostering calm behavior, you help them understand the appropriate times to exhibit self-control. This is particularly important for excitable puppies or dogs with high energy levels.

Training your dog to wait patiently before receiving rewards or before entering or exiting doorways helps reinforce self-discipline. By incorporating commands such as "sit" or "stay," you establish boundaries and encourage your dog to exercise self-restraint. This not only leads to more well-behaved behavior but also builds their self-confidence and reduces their frustration.

Creating an environment where your dog can calmly

respond to various stimuli is also essential. No treat dog training focuses on rewarding and reinforcing calm behavior, which can be particularly helpful during situations that may usually cause anxiety or excitement. With consistent training, your dog will learn to stay calm and composed, making everyday experiences more enjoyable for both of you.

COMMUNICATION

Clear and effective communication is the foundation of successful dog training, and no treat dog training places significant emphasis on improving communication between you and your furry friend. Understanding your dog's body language and improving your verbal and non-verbal cues can greatly enhance your ability to communicate effectively.

Dogs primarily communicate through body language, using their facial expressions, tail movements, and posture to convey their emotions and intentions. By observing and learning your dog's unique signals, you can better understand their needs, desires, and moods. No treat dog training encourages this level of attentiveness, fostering a deeper connection and improving your ability to respond appropriately to your dog's cues.

Improving your verbal cues, such as voice

commands and verbal praise, is another vital aspect of effective communication. Consistency and clarity in your commands help your dog understand what behaviors you're reinforcing. For example, saying a firm "No" when they exhibit undesirable behavior and immediately redirecting them to a more appropriate action reinforces the desired behavior and helps them learn from their mistakes.

CREATING A WELL-BEHAVED DOG

One of the primary objectives of dog training is to create a well-behaved and obedient companion. No treat dog training provides effective techniques for teaching your dog basic obedience commands, addressing behavior issues, and developing good manners.

Teaching basic obedience commands, such as "sit," "stay," and "come," is essential for establishing control and ensuring your dog's safety. Through positive reinforcement methods, you can teach your dog these commands without relying on treats. Consistency, patience, and rewarding desired behaviors with praise or playtime will help your pup understand and comply with your commands.

Addressing behavior issues is another critical aspect of dog training. Whether your dog exhibits excessive barking, jumping, or destructive behavior, no treat training enables you to correct and manage these issues effectively. Positive reinforcement techniques help redirect unwanted behaviors, reinforce more desirable actions, and promote a harmonious environment in your household.

Developing good manners is crucial for enhancing your dog's overall behavior and ensuring their compatibility with others. No treat dog training focuses on teaching your dog polite manners, such as not jumping on guests, walking calmly on a leash, and not begging for food. By consistently reinforcing positive behaviors and setting clear expectations, you can shape your dog's behavior to be courteous and well-mannered.

LONG-TERM BEHAVIOR MODIFICATION

No treat dog training goes beyond immediate behavior modification by promoting long-term changes in your dog's behavior. This approach addresses the root causes of behavioral issues rather than simply suppressing the symptoms, resulting in lasting transformations.

The emphasis on positive reinforcement methods helps change undesirable behaviors by replacing them with more appropriate alternatives. For example, if your dog exhibits fear-based aggression, the training would focus on building their confidence and teaching them alternative ways to cope with their fears. By rewarding calm behavior and gradually desensitizing them to the triggers, you can effectively modify their long-term behavior.

Additionally, no treat training techniques focus on preventing future behavior issues. By proactively addressing potential challenges, such as separation anxiety, resource guarding, or leash reactivity, you can lay the foundation for a well-adjusted and emotionally balanced dog. This preventive approach minimizes the likelihood of future problems, creating a more harmonious and stress-free environment for both you and your canine companion.

TAILORING TRAINING TO INDIVIDUAL DOGS

No treat dog training recognizes that each dog is unique, with different personality traits, learning styles, and breed characteristics. This approach allows for tailoring the training methods and techniques to suit your dog's specific needs, ensuring the highest level of effectiveness in the training process.

Considering breed characteristics is essential when designing a training program. Different breeds have distinct traits and tendencies, and understanding these traits allows you to address specific challenges more efficiently. For instance, some breeds are more stubborn and require more patience and consistency, while others are highly energetic and benefit from additional mental and physical stimulation.

Adapting to different learning styles is another aspect of individualized training. Dogs have various learning preferences, and while some may respond well to visual cues, others may be more receptive to verbal cues or physical demonstrations. By observing your dog's responses and tailoring your training methods accordingly, you can optimize their learning experience and achieve better results.

FOSTERING PROBLEM-SOLVING SKILLS

No treat dog training provides an opportunity for your dog to develop problem-solving skills and engage in cognitive activities. By incorporating puzzles, games, and interactive toys into the training process, you stimulate their mental abilities and encourage them to think and make decisions.

Engaging your dog in stimulating mental enrichment activities helps prevent boredom and provides an outlet for their natural instincts. For example, using treat-dispensing puzzle toys engages your dog's problem-solving abilities, as they have to figure out how to retrieve the treats by manipulating the toy. This mental stimulation keeps their minds sharp and satisfied, leading to a happier and more contented dog.

In addition to improving cognitive skills, problem-solving activities during training promote mental engagement and reduce the likelihood of behavioral issues caused by frustration or boredom. When your dog learns how to channel their energy into productive tasks, they are less likely to engage in destructive behaviors or exhibit excessive energy.

STRENGTHENING INDEPENDENCE

No treat dog training also focuses on strengthening your dog's independence and reducing separation anxiety. Dogs are social animals, and they often develop a strong attachment to their owners. While this bond is beautiful, it's also essential for your dog to feel comfortable and confident when left alone.

Through positive reinforcement methods, you can train your dog to feel secure and content even when you're not present. Gradually increasing the duration of their alone time and consistently rewarding calm behavior can help minimize separation anxiety. Building their independence allows you to leave your dog at home without worry, enhancing their overall well-being and your own peace of mind.

Reducing separation anxiety also leads to fewer destructive behaviors and excessive barking, promoting a healthier environment for both you and your neighbors. By strengthening your dog's independence, you enable them to be more resilient, adaptable, and relaxed in various situations.

NO TREAT TRAINING FOR FOOD-SENSITIVE DOGS

While treats are often a popular form of reward in dog training, some dogs have specific dietary requirements or food sensitivities that make traditional treat-based training challenging. No treat dog training offers alternative reward options that cater to dogs with food restrictions, ensuring they can still benefit from effective training methods.

Instead of using food rewards, you can substitute them with non-food rewards, such as verbal praise, affectionate petting, or playtime. The key is finding what motivates and excites your dog, whether it be a favorite toy, an opportunity to engage in a preferred activity, or a special outing. Understanding your dog's preferences and finding alternative rewards allows you to maintain motivation and reinforce desired behaviors without compromising their dietary needs.

Overcoming treat dependency is another advantage of no treat dog training. Some dogs can become overly reliant on treats, leading to challenges in phasing out the rewards once the behavior is established. No treat training allows for a more seamless transition from relying heavily on treats to emphasizing intrinsic rewards such as praise, play, or access to preferred activities. This creates a more sustainable and balanced training approach in the long run.

INSTILLING LIFELONG LEARNING SKILLS

No treat dog training promotes continuous learning throughout your dog's life. Training is not a one-time event but an ongoing process that develops skills and strengthens your bond over time. By adopting a mindset of lifelong learning, you can enrich your dog's life and provide them with new challenges and opportunities for growth.

Continuously engaging your dog in learning activities, whether it's teaching them advanced tricks, participating in agility courses, or exploring new environments, keeps their minds active and engaged. Dogs thrive on mental stimulation, and regular training sessions provide an outlet for their intelligence and curiosity.

Additionally, lifelong learning helps prevent

behavioral regression by reinforcing previously taught behaviors and introducing new ones. By incorporating training into your daily routines, you maintain a consistent and structured environment that enables your dog to continually build their skills and reinforce positive behaviors.

Efficient Time Management

No treat dog training offers the advantage of efficient time management by integrating training into your daily routines and activities. The flexibility of this training approach allows you to incorporate training moments seamlessly throughout the day, maximizing the use of your time and ensuring consistent reinforcement of desired behaviors.

For example, during feeding times, you can use portions of your dog's daily meals as rewards for training exercises. Instead of simply placing the food bowl down, you can use each mealtime as an opportunity to teach and reinforce commands, such as "sit" or "stay." This not only provides mental stimulation but also enhances their obedience skills and encourages a positive association with mealtime.

Incorporating training during daily walks is another

efficient way to utilize your time. Adding simple exercises, such as practicing loose leash walking or recall commands, turns a routine walk into a training session. These short bursts of training throughout the day contribute to your dog's overall learning and reinforce the behaviors you desire in different contexts.

By integrating training into your daily activities, you make the most of your time and create a consistent training environment that supports your dog's development.

PROMOTING A HAPPIER ENVIRONMENT

No treat dog training promotes a happier and more enjoyable environment for you, your dog, and everyone around you. By embracing positive reinforcement methods and focusing on building a strong bond, this training approach fosters a harmonious relationship and reduces stress and frustration.

The absence of punishment or aversive techniques in no treat training creates a positive atmosphere that encourages cooperation and mutual understanding. By reinforcing desirable behaviors and redirecting unwanted ones using positive methods, you build your dog's confidence and trust, leading to a happier and more willing participant in the training process.

Reduced frustration and stress are additional

benefits of no treat dog training. Dogs thrive on clear communication and consistent reinforcement of positive behaviors. This approach minimizes confusion and uncertainty, creating a stress-free environment that allows your dog to relax and enjoy the training process. As a result, you experience less frustration and enjoy a closer and more harmonious relationship with your furry friend.

CONCLUSION

No treat dog training and puppy training offer a plethora of benefits for both you and your canine companion. By adopting positive reinforcement techniques, you can build a strong bond, improve communication, and promote self-discipline in your dog. This approach fosters a well-behaved and well-adjusted canine companion, while also providing mental stimulation and promoting problem-solving skills.

With no treat training, you can tailor the training to suit your dog's individual needs, taking into account breed characteristics and learning styles. By focusing on long-term behavior modification and instilling lifelong learning skills, you create an environment that supports continuous growth and development.

Efficient time management and the ability to overcome treat dependency make this training approach practical and sustainable. Ultimately, no treat dog training promotes a happier and more enjoyable environment for both you and your furry friend, strengthening the bond and enhancing the overall quality of life.

.

FAQS (FREQUENTLY ASKED QUESTIONS)

1. Can No Treat Dog Training Be Used For All Breeds And Ages?

Yes, no treat dog training can be used for dogs of all breeds and ages. The principles of positive reinforcement apply universally, and the techniques can be adapted to suit different breeds and their specific needs.

2. Are Treats Completely Eliminated In No Treat Dog Training?

While the emphasis is on reducing reliance on treats, they are not completely eliminated. Treats may still be used occasionally or as a secondary form of reinforcement, especially for certain challenging behaviors or complex tasks.

3. How Long Does It Take To See Results With No Treat Dog Training?

The time it takes to see results can vary depending on the individual dog, their learning capabilities, and the specific behaviors being addressed. Consistency, patience, and positive reinforcement are key to achieving desired results.

4. Can I Combine No Treat Dog Training With Other Training Methods?

Yes, no treat dog training can be combined with other training methods as long as they are positive and reinforcement-based. However, it's important to ensure consistency and avoid confusion by using clear and consistent cues and rewards.

5. Can I Transition From Treat-Based Training To No Treat Dog Training With An Older Dog?

Yes, transitioning from treat-based training to no

treat dog training with an older dog is possible. While it may require more time and patience, the principles of positive reinforcement and communication can still be effective in modifying behavior and strengthening the bond with your older canine companion.

6. Can No Treat Dog Training Be Used For All Breeds And Ages?

Yes, no treat dog training can be used for dogs of all breeds and ages. The principles of positive reinforcement apply universally, and the techniques can be adapted to suit different breeds and their specific needs.

7. Are Treats Completely Eliminated In No Treat Dog Training?

While the emphasis is on reducing reliance on treats, they are not completely eliminated. Treats may still be used occasionally or as a secondary form of reinforcement, especially for certain challenging behaviors or complex tasks.

8. How Long Does It Take To See Results With No Treat Dog Training?

The time it takes to see results can vary depending on the individual dog, their learning capabilities, and the specific behaviors being addressed. Consistency, patience, and positive reinforcement are key to achieving desired results.

9. Can I Combine No Treat Dog Training With Other Training Methods?

Yes, no treat dog training can be combined with other training methods as long as they are positive and reinforcement-based. However, it's important to ensure consistency and avoid confusion by using clear and consistent cues and rewards.

10. Can I Transition From Treat-Based Training To No Treat Dog Training With An Older Dog?

Yes, transitioning from treat-based training to no

treat dog training with an older dog is possible. While it may require more time and patience, the principles of positive reinforcement and communication can still be effective in modifying behavior and strengthening the bond with your older canine companion.

We hope this article has provided valuable insights and guidance on the benefits of no treat dog training and its positive impact on your dog's behavior and well-being. Remember to approach the training process with patience, consistency, and love, and enjoy the journey of creating a happy and obedient companion.

www.ingramcontent.com/pod-product-compliance
Lightning Source LLC
Chambersburg PA
CBHW060902260726
48661CB00008B/3406